Gardening For Ent

GARDENING TECHNIQUES FOR HIGH YIELD HIGH PROFIT CROPS

Entrepreneur Publishing

Copyright

DISCLAIMER

FREE GIFT

Kindle 5 Star Books

Free Kindle 5 Star Book Club Membership

Join Other Kindle 5 Star Members Who Are Getting Private Access To Weekly Free Kindle Book Promotions

Get free Kindle books

Stay connected:

Join our Facebook group

Follow Kindle 5 Star on Twitter

Also, if you want to receive updates on Entrepreneur Publishing's new books, free promotions and Kindle countdown deals sign up to their New Release Mailing List.

For entrepreneurs: http://www.entrepreneurfinesse.com

TABLE OF CONTENTS

INTRODUCTION

With the frequent Google updates, making Internet marketing more challenging, more and more entrepreneurs are looking for ventures that provide offline real world opportunities. If you are bored of trying to outfox the search engines and compete with thousands of other online marketers, a real world enterprise could be just what you are looking for. Although many entrepreneurs may feel that the real world marketplace is overly competitive, there are still a great number of opportunities to be had.

While you may have had an interest in gardening, you may be unaware of the potential profits available from a gardening enterprise. Of course, gardening is not a simple get rich scheme and does require some dedication and hard work. However, unlike a flash in the pan phenomenon, where you need to be first onto the bandwagon, gardening can generate a substantial income for many years to come.

This book details the techniques you will need to employ to avoid rushing in to a costly mistake. While there is a temptation to just get out there with your watering can and a shovel, a gardening enterprise takes planning, preparation and proper investment. We will cover all the details you need to know from planning out your plot, choosing the right crops and the marketing techniques you can use to create a successful enterprise.

We provide tips and techniques that even those new to gardening can implement to begin their gardening venture. This includes minimizing costs to maximize profits, pricing strategies and selling to different markets.

Whether you are interested in growing flowers, organic vegetables or specialty crops, there is a market out there, just waiting for your produce. We will help you to harness this demand into a viable enterprise, which could generate an income every year for as long as you maintain it.

What are you waiting for? Get those green fingers to use and generate an income with your new gardening enterprise.

CHAPTER 1: The Principles of Gardening for Entrepreneurs

As more and more people become health conscious, there has been an increased demand for high quality organic produce. While many large farms may be struggling to make a profit in recent years, there is an emerging trend of people growing their own produce. This can be a great way to gain access to fresh organic produce and save money on household expenses. However, for innovative entrepreneurs there is still great opportunity to develop a great business strategy. Even in the challenging economic climate, there are a number of ways to develop a full or part time income. Gardening can be a great low entry level way to develop a profitable business, but before you contemplate beginning a gardening enterprise, there are some basic principles which you will need to consider.

Explore Specialist Items:

The first principle is that you will not be able to make a great profit growing basic items such as iceberg lettuce and tomatoes. You will need to explore more specialist and unusual fruits and vegetables, which can produce a high yield and will have a more demanding market. These items are often more hard to find, which allows them to command a premium price, providing greater profits for you.

Be Sure to Work Smarter Not Harder:

The second principle is that you will need to work smarter not harder. Although gardening can be backbreaking work, there is no need for you to spend all of your time laboring in your garden. Once you have established your garden, there are a number of methods and techniques, which can make your garden, lower maintenance, reducing the amount of work and labor needed during the growing season.

Use the Space You Have:

Another principle for entrepreneur gardening is that you don't need to use acres and acres of land. Preferably you will need at least an acre, but you can still turn a good profit even if you only have half an acre of land. More land does not necessarily mean more profit. If you can effectively and efficiently use the land, you can turn a great profit even on a smaller plot. This will involve planning ahead to determine the best types of crops to suit your climate, soil type and the amount of space.

Invest in the Best:

You will also need to be prepared to purchase the best bulbs, seeds, plants, trees and vines. There is no point in attempting to cut corners on this aspect of your enterprise. Buying substandard cheaper seeds could compromise the quality of your crop and prevent you from using the seeds for planting future crops. As with any enterprise, you will need to speculate to accumulate. Although the start up costs can be very low if you already own a plot of land, you will still need to be prepared to invest a couple of hundred dollars on quality seeds and starting materials.

Develop Your Marketing Skills:

Another principle of successful gardening for entrepreneurs is that you will need to harness your marketing skills. It is all very well to grow excellent produce, but you will not turn a profit if you cannot sell at the best possible price. Cash crops can be a low risk and low cost enterprise but you will need to be prepared to hone your marketing skills to showcase your fantastic produce.

CHAPTER 2: The Basics of Choosing Your High Yield Crops

One of the most important principles of gardening as a profitable enterprise is choosing the right crops. You could have the most fertile soil and the greatest marketing skills but if you are growing common items such as iceberg lettuce, you are unlikely to make a great profit. Therefore, it is well worth taking some time to research the best high yield crops that can generate a greater profit. There are a number of different types of crops that have great potential as an enterprise. These can be classified into a number of distinct groups.

Small Fruits:

Growing fruit can present a great opportunity even for a part time entrepreneur. Whether you live in an urban neighborhood or a large metropolitan city, chances are the area needs more producers, especially for small fruits. Some great examples of these are **strawberries, raspberries and blueberries**. These types of fruits will generally offer an excellent return on investment. Much of the demand for small fruits is generated for pick your own fields near to cities or urban neighborhoods.
This type of enterprise requires a few acres to grow your small fruits. However, it can offer a substantial income. With the exception of strawberries, most small fruit plants will produce fruit for up to ten years or more. This type of crop can produce a very high gross income per acre of up to $15,000.

Blueberries:

One example of this type of enterprise is blueberries. It is possible to fit approximately 1,000 of these small bushes on to an acre. Blueberries require an acidic soil and are arguably the best crop for a pick your own operation. You will need to be prepared for a little extra work as blueberries do take a little care and soil acidity management for optimum yield.

However, once your blueberries are established, they can command an excellent income.

Grapes:

Another example of great small fruit crops is grapes. Grape vines can be grown in almost any type of well-drained fertile soil. Vines can last for decades and allow you to produce a permanent income. You could use your grape crop as a pick your own enterprise or sell them via retail stores. You will need to learn the proper pruning techniques for your grapevines but there is plenty of information available including the Department of Agriculture website.

Raspberries:

Raspberries are a low cost investment for a good income. Raspberry plants produce fruit quickly and will produce for many years. These small fruits are easy to establish with few disease issues and will generally provide a large crop. Despite this ease of production, there are still supply problems to meet the great demand. This is great for entrepreneurs as raspberries can command a high price per quart and you can even add to your crop each year by propagating new plants from your existing stock. Raspberries have very low demands for soil conditions, simply requiring well-drained soil with plenty of sunshine and mulching.

Strawberries:

Another popular favorite crop are strawberries. You can sell your crop directly or create a pick your own enterprise. Despite the low cost of establishing a strawberry patch, you can obtain a yield of between 6,000 and 15,000 pounds of fruit per acre.

While there are plenty of lesser-known small fruits such as **guavas, kiwi fruit** or Chinese dates, new gardening entrepreneurs may wish to consider the above four cash crop fruits to begin their venture. If you are planning on developing a pick your own enterprise, you will need to consider that there will be some other start up costs, such as signage and parking for your customers. You may also wish to have portable restrooms for your customer use. You will also need reusable containers for each customer. This will allow you to sell per container rather than needing to weigh out fruit by the pound. You may also wish to have some form of schedule and send your pickers into assigned rows to avoid wastage. You will also need to create a relaxed family friendly atmosphere to help your customers enjoy themselves. Consider the odd piece of fruit eaten rather than put in the container, a cost of doing business.

Flowers:

When considering gardening as an enterprise, many people will overlook the tremendous profits available from flowers. Flower growing provides several opportunities to make a profit. You could sell cut flowers, flower plants or even sell bulbs. Flowers can be sold in a number of ways, both retail and wholesale. One of the most attractive features of growing flowers as an enterprise is that you can establish a good size business on less than half an acre of land. This makes flowers a great choice if space is limited.

According to the USDA producing flowers is the fastest growing form of agricultural business today. The supply of flowers is far outweighed by the demand, providing an amazing potential for even a new entrepreneur. Flowers have grown in popularity throughout the years and if you have a love for flowers this could be a fun way to make a profit while learning more about your interest.

A good method of growing flowers as a profitable enterprise is to build a greenhouse. This will allow you to grow plants for retail outlets to sell in the spring. Popular choices for cut flowers include **roses, snapdragons, carnations and chrysanthemums**. However, you may also wish to consider selling bulbs such as **lilies, tulips, irises crocuses and daffodils**, or live flowers such as **violets, roses and wildflowers**. Although a greenhouse may be a considerable investment, you should find that one good season will allow you to recoup your investment. Growing flowers does require a degree of knowledge, so you will need to be prepared to conduct some specialist research.

Herbs:

Another great crop for entrepreneurs are herbs. Herbs can be divided into three basic groups; culinary, medicinal and fragrant. Some herbs may fit into more than one of the groups. Culinary herbs are used as food or a seasoning, medicinal herbs are used in herbal remedies and alternative medicine and fragrant herbs are used for potpourri and scents. The demand for herbs is increasing in today's market, with demand far outstripping the domestic supply. This provides a great opportunity for entrepreneurs to create a profitable venture. An herb growing business can be started with a small amount of space yet provide a substantial income. This can generate a decent return per acre of up to $15,000. Herbs are also very hardy and can be grown on almost every type of soil and area of the United States. Additionally, herbs can deliver a fast return as your crop can produce an income in the first year of planting.

There are a great number of resources available to help you with the planting and growing of herbs, including gardening magazines. You can sell your herbs direct to customers as a plant, direct as a finished herb product, wholesale to retail stores, bulk herb buyers, arts and crafts people, or direct to restaurants.

The first step to generating a profitable herb growing venture is to determine which herbs you will grow. Some herbs require special conditions to flourish, so you will need to check which ones are suited to your particular location and soil conditions.

Successful growers will typically grow a selection of different herbs. This will allow you to diversify your income potential. For example, *you could choose to grow several different culinary herbs to sell to restaurants, a number of fragrant herbs for marketing to the arts and crafts crows and a couple of medicinal herbs for direct customer sales*. You can even develop a mail order business selling dried herbs. It is a good idea to concentrate your efforts to growing one or two varieties of big demand herbs, for example catnip and peppermint. However, before you invest in specializing, you will need to ensure that you research your selling options and even arrange for some contracts with buyers.

Vegetables:

There is a constant demand for home grown fresh vegetables. Often, you will be able to obtain a great profit margin while beating large supermarket chains on both price and quality. You could even supply your small grocery stores. However, the largest profit margins come from direct retail sales from customers looking for chemical free, fresh produce.

There are quite literally dozens of different crops of vegetables you can grow to produce a substantial profit. Ideally, you should choose to grow eight to ten varieties of popular vegetables. Intensive growing techniques will allow you to increase the yield of produce per acre, to increase your potential profits of up to $20,000 per acre.

Some suggestions for popular vegetables include;

Asparagus:
This can offer a yield of up to 2,000 pounds on an acre with a retail price of $2 per pound. The plant is started as a root and will be ready to use in approximately three years. However, the plant will continue to produce for up to twenty years.

Beans:
Beans are always a popular crop and there are plenty of easy to grow options. Beans will typically produce several crops per growing season.

Baby carrots:
With a strong demand, baby carrots are relatively easy to grow in loose fertile soil, yet can offer a decent return on your investment.

Lettuce:
Although lettuce is simple and quick to grow, there are a number of varieties that command a higher level of consumer demand. Lettuce can be planted early and offer several harvests throughout the growing season.

Peppers:

Peppers can be grown in both mild and hot varieties. Peppers require well-drained soil and a long warm growing season. However, there is plenty of consumer demand including groups who specialize in enjoying the very hot varieties.

You can market your home grown vegetables in a number of different ways. You could choose to arrange a pick your own venture but one of the most profitable methods is to have a small roadside stand or stall at a farmers market. You can also sell your produce directly to local stores, food co-ops and restaurants. If you want to optimize your profits, you will need to ensure that your produce is organic and chemical free. This does require a little more effort and soil preparation but the booming market demand will allow you to obtain premium profits.

Specialty Crops:

There are also a number of specialist cash crops, which can deliver great profits. Many of these types of crops will require particular growing conditions and can only be grown in certain areas of the country. These specialty crops include;

Bamboo:
Bamboo is a popular material for the construction of furniture and other accessories, and for edible shoots. Currently, the demand for bamboo far outstrips supply and most bamboo is imported into the country. However, bamboo offers a very high yield of up to ten tons per acre.

Dried Flower and Plants:
Dried plants have a wide number of markets including arts and crafts, gift stores and florists. You will need to grow a very attractive high quality plant and dry it using the proper methods, to ensure optimum price from your buyer.

Landscaping and Decorative Plants:
Landscaping plants are always in demand and include decorative trees and shrubs such as juniper, azalea and rhododendron. These can be sold to consumers directly or to landscaping companies. Supplying retail outlets or

landscaping companies with a reasonable amount of stock can offer a steady income. However, before you consider growing landscaping plants, you should be aware that the plants must have a good rate of survival and look attractive. You may also need to offer some sort of guarantee that your plants are disease free.

Mushrooms:

Growing mushrooms can also be a very profitable venture. Many varieties of mushrooms are considered a specialty for both home cooking enthusiasts and restaurants. Shiitake mushrooms are especially suited to small farm growing. This variety of mushroom offers a meaty flavor and can also be used for medicinal purposes. Shiitake can be harvested in spring and fall, and are typically grown on logs outdoors. The logs are specially prepared and inoculated with mushroom spores. The first crop is usually available for harvesting within six to eight months. However, there are some indoor varieties that offer a shorter growing season.

Another popular variety is the oyster mushroom. This variety of mushroom is fast growing and offers a high yield. They are typically grown on wheat straw and can be marketed as a fresh or dried product for restaurants, health food stores, grocers or direct customer sales.

Nuts:

Nut crops can be a long-term investment but are well worth the wait. Varieties including pecans, walnuts, chestnuts and almonds can mean a wait of up to twenty years for production. However, you could sell aged trees for replanting, with two or three year old trees commanding a premium price. Nut trees can take time to mature and produce a crop, but they can be a valuable asset for lumber production for up to thirty years. This means that nuts could be an excellent retirement crop with black walnut trees in particular commanding up to $10,000 each. Since there is such a long wait for a crop, most growers will dual grow, planting a small fruit crop between trees for an optimum use of the space.

Seeds:

Seeds are also another profitable specialist crop. With many people concerned about GMO seeds and crops, a great number will pay a premium for high quality seeds. Your choice of seeds includes flowers, wildflowers, fruits and vegetables. These can be sold directly to consumers or to local garden centers and retailers.

Obviously the size of the plot will dictate your choice of crops and the particular layout of your growing space. If your plot is less than an acre, you are likely to be best suited to choosing crops, which can generate a large amount of produce from a smaller space. Fruit and other tree varieties should only be considered if you have significant acreage. However, even if you are considering gardening as an enterprise on a smaller plot, there are plenty of options for profitable crops. Your choice of crop will depend greatly on your personal preferences, interests and location. How you intend to market the produce and whether it can only be sold locally or has national sales potential may also determine it. Therefore, it is important to take some time to research your options and properly plan out your crop and your space. This will allow you to avoid wastage and optimize profits.

CHAPTER 3: Planning Your Enterprise

As with any entrepreneurial venture, proper planning is the key to success. While you may have a yearning to grow a particular crop, your type of soil, geography and even the size of the plot may limit you. Therefore, it is important to take time out to plan your plot for high yield profits.

Take Time to Develop Your Soil:

The first step in planning your new enterprise is to consider your soil. You will need to assess the type of soil and determine whether it is compatible with your choice of crop. In most cases, you will still need to build up the soil to increase nutrients and boost your potential yield. Organically rich deep soil is the key to encouraging extensive and healthy roots, which can reach more water and nutrients. This can help to generate extra lush and productive growth above the ground. This need not be difficult and does not require the use of chemicals. Natural fertilizers can provide a great way to boost the nutrients in your soil. Chicken, horse or cow manure can allow you to eliminate the use of chemical fertilizer products and allow you to keep your crops organic. This can immediately increase interest and demand in your produce as most store bought produce is either grown using chemicals or very overpriced as organic.

A long term consideration to keep your soil lush is to start a composting area on your land. This allows you to turn any leaves, clippings and other organic material into a rich soil. Composting need not be complicated and you can simply start a pile in one corner of your plot by layering up four or five inches of leaves with an inch or two of dirt and some manure. This can be repeated until the pile is up to four feet tall. If your climate is particularly dry, lightly sprinkle every layer with water. Some growers find it more beneficial to create a wire mesh box to contain the pile. You can either leave the pile alone for eight or nine months or speed the composting process by mixing the pile every five to seven days. The compost is ready to be worked into your soil when it resembles a rich soil mixture.

If you are unsure about the exact nature of your soil, it is a good idea to have it tested. This will allow you to know whether the soil is acid or alkaline and the mineral content. Knowing the exact specifications of your soil will allow you to tailor your crops accordingly or take action to adjust the soil conditions. The more care you take preparing the soil, the better your results are likely to be.

Consider Raised Beds:

One technique you may wish to consider is establishing raised beds. Typically a raised bed can generate up to four times the yield of planted rows in the same space. This is not just because of the fertile loose soil but because you can efficiently plan your space. You will use less space for pathways, leaving more growth room. Raised beds can also save you time as planting and maintaining a bed can be accomplished in less time yet deliver a greater yield. The close spacing of raised beds allows you to shade out weeds and more efficiently water your plants, making planting, care and harvesting much easier.

If you are considering using raised beds on your plot, you will also need to think about the shape. Research has shown that rounded tops on your beds to create an arc is actually more space efficient than squared off shapes. A raised bed five feet wide at the base will create a six-foot wide arc at the top. This can make a great difference in the amount of planting space and could add up to twenty percent capacity.

Plan Out Your Planting:

Another consideration for planning your plot is to work out the arrangement of your plants. Effective planning of your space can have a dramatic effect on the size of your yield. Rather than planting in straight rows, consider planting in triangles, staggering the plants. This will allow you to increase the number of plants by approximately ten percent. However, you should avoid planting too tightly as you may stunt potential growth and prevent the plants from reaching their full size. For example, lettuces can double in size if you increase spacing between plants from eight to ten inches. Packing your plants in too tightly can also trigger stress in the plants, which makes them susceptible to insect attacks and disease.

Consider Vertical Gardening:

Smaller plots can also benefit from planning vertical gardening techniques. Vining crops will generally prefer growing straight upwards, but it is also possible to make the most of your space with small fruits and leafy crops being grown vertically. Vertical growing can also save time on maintenance and harvesting, and reduce the risk of fungal disease due to the increased circulation of air.

Plan for Compatible Crops:

When planning out your plot, it is a good idea to consider interplanting a number of compatible crops. This can save space and increase your potential profits. For example, a classic combination is the Native American "three sisters". This involves companion growing of beans, squash and corn. The cornstalks provide support for the beans, while the space along the ground provides plenty of room for the squash while shading out weeds. Other good combinations include lettuce, peas and brassicas or carrots, onions and radish.

Allow for Succession Planting:

Another factor for your planning is to consider succession planning. This allows you to maximize the available space with more than one crop being produced during the growing season. Successful implementation of succession growing techniques could allow you to harvest up to four crops from one area. In order to optimize this potential, you should use transplants rather than seeded plants. Transplants are a month old to prompt faster maturity. You should also choose varieties of plants, which are fast maturing and keep the soil replenished with compost worked into the top of the soil for every replant.

Extend Your Growing Season:

You can also plan out an extended growing season by considering keeping a warm air around plants during colder weather. This can be accomplished using covers, cloches, mulching or even a cold frame. This can allow you to add a few weeks to the end of the growing season, allowing another harvest of a fast growing crop such as lettuce or spinach. You can also plan to use this technique to create an early start for your heat loving plants such as peppers. You can preheat cold soil approximately six to eight weeks before the date of the last frost, with black plastic or mulch.

Get The Plan Down On Paper:

All of these considerations can be a little overwhelming, so it is a good idea to sit down with a pencil and paper to plan out your plot. Create a rough to scale outline of your plot and determine what area is required for optimum yield. Unless you have a confirmed contract for a large amount of one particular plant, it is a good idea to choose eight to ten different plants. Therefore, you can plan out which areas would be most beneficial for particular varieties. You should consider the limitations of your plot, which may affect certain plants. For example, you may have a particularly shaded spot along a fence line or an area prone to collecting water. These areas should be reserved for more hardy plants, which can withstand the conditions. If you are considering raised beds or vertical growing techniques, you can plan out your plot layout for maximum yield. Remember that fence lines and buildings can provide a good source of support for vertical gardening.

Getting a plan for your plot down on paper can help you to assess your objectives. For example, you may find that your plan of exclusively growing raspberries is not feasible due to a lack of sunlight around the perimeter of your plot. However, this is an opportunity to plan out an alternative strategy. For example, you may vary up your plot with leafy vegetables, which could scorch in full sun, or root vegetables that only require a few hours of sun each day for optimum growth.

Planning out your plot can be a quick and easy way to save money, before you invest in seeds or plants. You will need to realistically check the physical location of your plot to determine its characteristics. This can avoid you investing in crops, which will not deliver a high yield from your particular plot.

CHAPTER 4: Top Tips to Maximize Your Yield and Profits

Maximizing your harvest is not simply a matter of luck and there are a number of tips and tricks that may help.

Start With the Best Seeds:

The first tip to maximize your harvest is to use the best possible seeds. As with any enterprise, if you have poor quality materials, you are going to struggle to make the best possible profit. You will need to research your seed source to determine that they are not GMO and of the highest quality. Heirloom seeds will allow you to collect your own seeds from the last of the crop for planting next season. Don't be tempted to cut corners with cheap seeds.

Be Patient:

Like an expectant parent, your first season of gardening as an enterprise is likely to involve spending time watching the growth and trying to "care" for your plants to encourage a greater yield. Unfortunately, over watering and over fertilizing can be a great problem among the inexperienced grower and could compromise your harvest. If you imagine your venture as a people based enterprise, while watering and fertilizing is essential, overdoing it is like giving your employees too much responsibility. As any experienced manager will tell you, your employees can only grow as quickly as they're naturally able. Your plants must go through their natural growth season for optimum results. While there may not be a great deal of stuff happening above ground, your plants are building their root system and too much care could result in you drowning or burning your plants out.

Familiarize Yourself With the Terminology:

One of the most important aspects of learning to grow for a profit is to learn the terminology. For example, the difference between a full sun and a partial sun can make the difference between a healthy crop and a withered set of plants. While this is important for any gardener, an amateur will be frustrated with a mistake but move on, but an entrepreneur could see their profits compromised and investment lost. As discussed in the previous chapter, planning the location of your plants is the key to success, but if you fail to understand the terminology, you are doomed to make costly mistakes.

Keep Thinking Organic:

While many entrepreneurs will understand that organic produce will provide a premium price, when faced with a problem such as an insect attack, these aims will go out of the window. However, a quick fix pesticide or chemical product will compromise the quality of your product and the potential profit of your yield. It is well worth taking a little time to research an organic solution to address the problem. In fact, it is a good idea to conduct your research on issues common to your area and chosen crop before a problem strikes. This will enable you to quickly correct any problems before they cause too much damage. For example, planting catnip has been shown to reduce the damage from flea beetles to collards. Other organic pest control methods include sticky traps, oil sprays, pheromone traps and plant covers. While organic pest control methods can be a little more creative and potentially a little more time consuming, it is well worth keeping organic. This does require a little advance planning but can optimize your yield without compromising on quality. Cutting corners and resorting to a chemical pest control, fertilizer or feed, will prevent you from marketing your produce as organic and immediately reduce your return. With organic produce generally costing up to thirty percent more than its chemically treated counterparts, you will need to carefully consider your options and ensure that you make the most profitable choice.

Consider Perennials:

While the initial cost may be more, it is worth assessing the financial benefit of planting perennial plants. Although some people may be after a quick buck, the serious entrepreneur understands that a growing venture can be a serious long-term income, if you lay the proper groundwork. For example, while lettuces are a quick to grow and easy crop to manage, establishing a raspberry plot can represent a much greater potential profit in the long term. Your lettuces will require minimal initial investment but once the harvest is over, you will be starting over from scratch next year. However, your raspberry plants will continue to produce fruit each year for years and years. This means that your return on investment will be far greater in the long term. Perennials will also reduce the time needed for your plot as you will only need to maintain your plot, rather than preparing the ground and replanting each year.

Research High Yield Varieties and Crops:

One of the most disappointing aspects of growing is to spend time and resources on a plant, only to find that it produces minimal results. While some element of plant failure is to be expected, you can mitigate this by choosing a high yielding variety. It is worth consulting local gardeners and growers for their expertise on which varieties can offer the best results in your particular area. It is worth considering traditionally bred, classic hybrid varieties, in addition, to open pollinated options. For example, when growing sweet peppers, you are likely to need the fast maturation and resistance to disease offered by hybrid varieties to produce a good crop. However, lettuce, peas, beans and winter squash often don't require hybridization to achieve optimum productivity.

Don't Specialize Early:

Although there is a temptation to find a great crop and stick with it, for the new growing entrepreneur, this can be a big risk. Each type of crop has their own particular requirements and if something unforeseen occurs such as adverse weather conditions, you could lose your entire crop. However, if you diversify a little, you can mitigate this risk. New entrepreneurs should choose eight to ten different plants to establish an enterprise and balance any risk. There is nothing to stop you growing plants, which complement each other. For example, if you want to establish a pick your own venture, why not offer several varieties of blueberries, raspberries and strawberries.

Grow From Seedlings Rather Than Seed:

If you wish to make the most of the space and growing season, you will need to grow from seedling. Seedlings will be quicker to mature and you can have your next set of seedlings developing while you are beginning to harvest your first crop. Seedlings can also be used to plug in any gaps in the plot around plants, which are almost at maturity. This form of relay planting allows you to tighten up your timing of succession planting and increase your potential yield over the same growing season.

CHAPTER 5: Planning a Smarter Harvest

For new growing entrepreneurs, one of the most challenging aspects of the venture is harvesting. This can be a make or break moment as you determine exactly what size yield you have produced. However, there are number of ways to have a smarter harvest to make the process simpler and ensure a high quality product which will command a premium price.

Pick at the Right Time:

The first aspect you will need to consider is that you only pick when the produce is at its peak. Generally, picking your harvest in the morning will ensure that the plants are plumped with moisture and nutrients. This will add to the flavor and the aesthetic appearance of your produce. Root vegetables, leafy greens and a number of other vegetables should be chilled to preserve the nutritional content and flavor. However, avoid refrigerating sweet potatoes and onions.

Pick Early and Frequently:

To maximize your yield, it is a good idea to pick your crop early and frequently. Many vegetables should be harvested when they are technically immature. If left too long, they may bolt and begin to flower, compromising the flavor and quality of the produce. However, when you harvest early produce frequently, you encourage the plants to stay in its reproduction mode for longer. This can allow an increased yield. For example, research from the University of Idaho Extension found that the daily harvesting of baby summer squash generated double the yield compared to the same varieties picked every three days. You should also consider that many fruits and vegetables such as peppers and tomatoes will continue to ripen after they have been harvested. This means that you can pick greener tomatoes or peppers and they will still ripen up to perfection for your customers.

Consider Cut and Come Again:

Another interesting aspect of harvesting is using cut and come again produce. Leafy greens such as spinach, chard and kale will actually regrow after each time you harvest. This provides the opportunity for two or three comebacks of produce if you create the opportunity. If you cut cabbages, broccoli and some other cruciferous vegetables high, you may find that it grows a small secondary head. Additionally, if you gently harvest bush beans, you are likely to find the plant offers two or three flushes of blooms and pods.

Take Root Cuttings:

You should also consider taking root cuttings during harvesting. Replanting the rooted bottom of your plants can provide you with a brand new plant in a short growing period. This could allow you to take root cuttings in early summer and have an early fall crop.

Don't Forget to Save Seeds:

One of the most exciting aspects of a growing enterprise is that you hold the potential for expansion without great financial reinvestment. If you have started your venture with the best quality seeds, you can collect and save seeds from your produce to use next season. While there is a temptation to sell every scrap of produce, you will need to remember to save some back during harvesting specifically for seeds. Collecting seeds from fruits is relatively simple and just requires the seeds to be cleaned, dried and possibly fermented to avoid disease. However, many vegetables will need to be allowed to over ripen to allow seeds to develop. This means leaving a few squash, eggplant or cucumbers on the vine, or leave a healthy shoot or two on your broccoli or several heads of cabbages and cauliflowers to allow seeds to develop. This may seem like a waste, but even a dozen items of produce could represent enough seeds for next year, so it is well worth learning seeding techniques for future growth.

Watch for Harvesting Needs on Pick Your Own Plots:

While having a pick your own plot can eliminate many of the harvesting work, it will still take some organization. After all, you are not going to have very happy customers if they arrive to pick and your fruit is not at its best. You will need to keep a plan of which rows should have ripened first and ensure that these are picked first by your customers. You will also need to space out your pickers, so that you don't have fruit over ripening and falling from the plants while others are lacking easy to find fruit. You will need to adequately market your pick your own venture to ensure that you get your customers at the right time. However, if customers are lacking and the fruit is at its best, it can be worthwhile to harvest some of the particularly ripe fruit. These can always be sold by the carton to customers who want delicious organic produce but are not bothered about picking their own.

Be Prepared to Learn:

As with every aspect of a growing enterprise, the more experience you have the easier, you will find harvesting. As you become an expert on your chosen crops, you will gain a feeling for when you can anticipate harvesting. If you are unsure about the growing seasons or harvesting periods for your specific produce, it is worth consulting a gardener's almanac, the particular seed variety instructions or local growing expert for further guidance.

CHAPTER 6: TECHNIQUES TO BALANCE YOUR TIME AND INVESTMENT

As any entrepreneur understands - time is money. If your growing venture takes up hours and hours each week throughout the whole growing season, your rate of return is diminished. However, it is possible to work smarter not harder and minimize your costs while maximizing your time efficiency.

For example, you can use a spade and fork to prepare your plot for planting. However, even on a half-acre plot this technique will take you several days of backbreaking work. It is a more sensible approach to hire a rototiller or pay someone with a tractor to plow the plot. This will save you a great deal of time for a very small amount of money.

Consider Companion Planting:

Obviously, you are likely to want to minimize your costs for the enterprise to maximize your potential profits. However, some initial savings could mean that you end up working far harder throughout the growing season. For example, while building and preparing raised beds is more time consuming and costly than simply planting in rows, raised beds can make maintenance such as weeding, watering and harvesting far easier taking up less time. You are also likely to find that raised beds will allow you to generate a higher yield, increasing profits. Another example, is taking the time to companion plant.

Planting flowers may seem like a costly waste of time when you are planning on growing vegetables, but certain pairings of plants can minimize the risk of damage from insects. This allows you to minimize loss and maintain a higher quality product, which will command a premium price, without needing to resort to chemical treatments. While this is an important aspect of planning out your plot, you must also be prepared to invest a little to avoid time inefficiency during the year. Imagine the time you would need to spend treating an insect infestation, while you watch your crop become damaged and lower quality. It is this balance of investment over time, which will help you to ensure a successful enterprise.

Mulch:

Again, mulching is a task, which can seem like a costly investment in time and resources. However, mulching can be a great way to prevent weeds from appearing in your crop. Mulch can smother any existing weeds, killing them off and removing the need to spend time pulling them. Additionally, a couple of inches of mulch will help to hold water in the soil, reducing the need and expense of frequent watering.

Get Help:

Another aspect of time versus investment is when you consider employing help. Whether you have a small or larger plot, chances are your high yield crop will be ready for harvesting at the same time. This means you face a choice of leaving your produce to potentially over ripen and spoil while you harvest by yourself or hire some help. However, this type of help need not be very expensive. Part time help such as students can be very reasonable and could allow you to harvest quickly. This speed could also help you to get another crop established and increase the total yield for the growing season.

Be Realistic:

It is important to remember, that if you are trying to keep your investment low for a new enterprise, you may have to compromise your ambitions. Rather than attempting a large-scale operation, it could be a good idea to start smaller with an area size you are comfortable with. This will allow you to develop your skills, market and customer demand. You can always expand as your confidence grows and you have more time available.

CHAPTER 7: Marketing Tips and Strategies for Your Growing Enterprise

In most cases, the amount of profit your growing enterprise can generate will come down to two factors; the quality of your produce and how you market it. With earnings per acre varying from $2,000 to $20,000 for a year, this type of venture can provide a serious income and a long-term enterprise. However, while you may be able to sell lower quality produce with fantastic marketing skills, if your marketing techniques are lacking, you are likely to struggle to sell even the most amazing produce. This means that learning some new marketing skills to sell your crops should be a priority. Fortunately, there are a number of strategies, which can help you and may influence the type of crops you wish to grow.

Essential Factors for Easier Marketing:

The techniques for selling your produce can vary and some growers will often use a number of methods simultaneously for optimum results. However, regardless of your marketing approach, there are several factors that you will need to consider.

Quality:

The first of these considerations is the quality of your product. You may be the type of salesperson who can sell sand in the desert, but having a good quality product makes sales far easier. You need to ensure that you produce the best possible product, Your produce should look healthy and clean to appeal to potential buyers. Sub-standard produce is far harder to sell and will group you with "ordinary" produce available at the local branch of a grocery store chain. This means that you will need to follow the planning, preparation and techniques detailed earlier in this book to produce the highest possible quality.

You will also want to take proactive action to eliminate any pests which could damage your plants and produce. This could include using natural pest repellents such as basil, garlic, thyme, catnip, marigolds and tansy or learning organic pest treatments such as orange oil. Part of your marketing strategy will need to be dedicated to research, from looking at customer demand through to learning accepted growing methods and techniques. This will make your overall marketing easier as you can have confidence in the quality of your product.

Timing:

Another important consideration for your marketing strategy is your timing. If you are able to produce a crop when other producers are still waiting to harvest, obtaining sales can be easy. This could involve using greenhouses, extending your growing season and planting early. You don't want to be late to the party on a time sensitive crop. For example, Brussels sprout growers are going to be out of luck if their crop is only ready to be harvested on December 26th. Therefore, you need to plan your crop properly to ensure that it is ready when you need it to get those sales.

Pricing:

The price at which you market your produce is also an important factor. Most growers will price their produce at up to twenty percent less than grocery stores. However, don't attempt to undercut the price of other small producers, as you may end up locked into a pricing war. Organic produce will automatically command a premium price, so compare local retail stores, other sellers and farmers markets to check out the current local selling rate.

Selling to a Specific Market:

Once you are confident of your quality, timing and price, you will need to get your produce to potential customers. This can be accomplished in a number of ways depending on your target market.

Selling Direct to the Public:

The most common technique to market your produce is selling your products at a roadside stand. However, before you consider this technique you should consider whether there is ample parking space and that you have adequate signage. Your signs need to be placed far enough away from the actual stand to allow drivers time to slow down and pull in. The signs should be clear and easy to understand with no more than seven or eight words. Don't make the sign so bright that it isn't legible and keep it looking professional.

You will need to organize your stand so that it has a neat appearance. Customers should be able to see the produce and prices easily. This care and attention is sure to pay off when combined with good prices and quality produce as "word of mouth" will provide a great deal of free advertising. If you don't want to invest in a stand initially, the same technique can be applied if you sell from the back of your car or pickup truck.

Another approach to sell your products is a farmer's market. Most areas have a schedule of regular farmer's markets to allow you to sell your organic produce. If your area does not have a market, you may wish to invest the time with other producers in your area to organize one.

The pick your own strategy is also another excellent method of marketing directly to the public. You can advertise in local newspapers, bulletin boards, community newsletters and websites. Don't forget to put up signage for your plot and plan out plenty of parking and customer amenities such as temporary toilets. Many of your potential customers will view a pick your own plot as a family event, so be prepared for small children to arrive with their parents by ensuring the site is safe from any hazardous tools and materials. You may wish to implement certain rules about small children if you are concerned about damage to crops or potential injury. Be aware that adverse weather will mean that your customers will not want to spend time outside picking, so be sure to advertise that you also sell by the container on site.

A successful pick your own venture requires you to have great people skills, as every visitor needs to be treated as an important customer. One aspect of a pick your own operation, you will need to accept as a cost of doing business, is that a large percentage of your customers will be sampling the merchandise. Children especially will be prone to popping fruit in their mouth rather than the container. This should be viewed as a good-natured goodwill gesture unless it becomes particularly problematic. Some humorous signs informing customers that fruit should go in the container, not the mouth, will usually do the trick.

Selling to Restaurants:

Restaurant management and chefs are always in need of good quality produce. If you are able to provide restaurants with steady supplies of fresh organic produce, you are likely to find plenty of customers. When considering selling to restaurants, seeing is believing. While some restaurants will discuss potential purchases over the phone, often showing the quality of your produce is a more effective marketing approach. Don't visit the restaurant during lunch or dinner service, but rather go when they have time to speak to you and check out what you have to offer. You are likely to need to give some assurances about the frequency and volume of produce before restaurants will switch suppliers, but if you can offer a discount and high quality produce, most will give you a try. Be sure to nurture these relationships and deliver as agreed for long-term profits and success.

Selling to Retailers:

Selling your produce to retailers can be another excellent way to market your venture. When you contact stores and retailers, you will need to be prepared to offer a discount of up to forty percent from the typical retail prices. This will create an attractive profit margin for most stores. If you can demonstrate reliability, you may be able to offer a weekly route between a number of retail locations. If your harvest is likely to provide a more bulk amount of produce, you could consider a food co-op.

Co-ops are more able and eager to consider a large quantity of good quality produce. You will need to be prepared to offer a reasonable discount to attract interest. Most co-ops will require you to contact them directly and you may need to prepare packages of your produce rather than a bulk load. For example, herbs are more attractive in one or two ounce labeled bags.

Internet Sales:

For most modern day entrepreneurs, the Internet provides a great marketplace and for certain types of gardening can offer a great sales opportunity. If you are selling specialist items, which have a national demand, you could market your items online. For example, there are a number of growers offering unusual types of mushrooms by next day mail order online. Many consumers will pay a premium for this convenience, especially if the item is not available for them locally. This is obviously not practical for larger vegetable items, which are readily available in most areas. Additionally, although there are next day courier services available, the appeal of most of your produce will be that it is local and fresh.

However, if you are planning on selling dried items such as flowers or herbs, there could be an online demand for your items, in fact certain specialist items have a greater demand for dried products such as mushrooms. Therefore, you may find it more profitable to dry your mushrooms and offer them for sale nationally rather than selling them fresh locally.

Selling a Finished Product:

Another marketplace for your items could be selling a finished product to the public or to retailers. For example, you could create a range of baked goods made using your organic produce. This is a more intensive enterprise and would be subject to more rigorous local and state laws. However, there have been a number of brands, which have emerged from a small enterprise making cakes, muffins, cookies or baby food with organic fresh produce. This can be especially profitable if you are able to appeal to a niche market such as vegetarians or vegans, dieters or the health conscious. Other entrepreneurs have developed full businesses based on their own organic produce. For example, if you have always dreamed of owning your own restaurant or cafe, your fresh organic produce could provide the cornerstone of your appeal.

CONCLUSION

Gardening can be a very satisfying hobby, but it can also provide the foundation of a very profitable enterprise. While it can take some experience and practice to develop the massive profits some entrepreneurs have created, even new gardeners can generate a respectable income and a significant return on their investment. While this book does provide strategies, techniques and tips, the outcome of your enterprise will depend greatly on your particular geographical location, plot and efforts.

It is therefore, important to research your gardening options to determine the ones best suited to you. There are plenty of resources available to assist you with gardening techniques and choosing crops for your specific area. These resources are available both on and offline, including the American Horticultural Association and other national, community and local groups. There are also local growers and enthusiasts who can supply a wealth of knowledge and experience to assist you in establishing and maintaining your enterprise.

While you may not necessarily have the resources and investment to start a massive enterprise, the great thing about a gardening venture is that it can grow over time. You may begin with only half an acre, but as you create your own seeds and take plant cuttings, you will be able to stock a larger plot without significant financial investment. This means that over time, you could create a larger enterprise, which can generate even greater profits year on year. Your small little part time venture could end up providing you a retirement income or a legacy to pass on to your children and grandchildren. While trends and fads come and go, human beings will always appreciate good quality produce and beautiful flowers or landscaping plants. This means that demand for your produce will continue to grow and grow. This can provide some reassurance that your venture has long term potential to generate a great income in the years to come.

I hope this book was able to help you to determine the viability of gardening for entrepreneurs. I wish you every success with your new enterprise and am sure that you will be able to generate great profits and a great return on your investment of both time and money. Happy gardening.

To hear about Entrepreneur Publishing's new books first (and to be notified when there are free promotions), sign up to their New Release Mailing List.

Finally, if you enjoyed this book, please take the time to share your thoughts and post a review on Amazon. It'd be greatly appreciated!

Thank you and good luck!

Preview Of 'How To Write A Book And Publish On Amazon' from Entrepreneur Publishing

WRITING YOUR CONTENT

Before you can think about publishing, first you must create your content. This can be very easy or very hard, depending on the level of content you want to produce. If you have already produced some of your content, such as through blog posts or forum comments, it can be as simple as pulling the content together and putting it into a readable format. However, if you are starting off from scratch, this could take a while.

Creating content is simple. You choose a topic, do your research if there is any, write your content, and then publish it. However, the sticky part is often: do your research. This can take up quite a lot of time, especially if you want to insure your piece is exhaustively researched. Otherwise, if you are writing something such as fiction or nonfiction that you are well versed in, the path is quite a bit simpler. You pick out your topic and write your content.

For example, say you are writing a romance novel. The most you would need to know is how a romance typically goes and what the target word count is for your project. Then you can simply write away. However, if you're writing a historical romance novel, things can become a little stickier as you have to worry about being historically accurate to a certain degree. No plastic buttons on the dress, please.

The actual process of writing can be very systematic. In a lot of cases, it means to basically just sit down and write even if the terror of the blank page can be too much to handle. When starting out you may wish to sit down and first outline what you would like to talk about and take a few notes either from your head or from your research to help you get that first page started. This is a good way to start any book, first decide what you want to say and what category it falls in.

For example, this book works on publishing for the entrepreneurial minded. The reader wants to get their work out there in the eyes of the public. It has a slightly different bent from a book on publishing written solely for the fiction market. Once you decide on subject matter and category, a few notes are in order to bring forth the best ideas for you to cover in writing your content. These notes are your brainstorming session, so don't worry if they're not completely functional. You want to get your ideas down on paper so that they will be there when you're ready to get started.

Take the time to write out your notes. You can always edit them into shape later if you need to, but at first the trick is to just get them out there. You can do this by free writing. Free writing is when you start to write without an end in mind and simply allow your mind to go where it wishes to go. It can offer some great insights into what you really want to talk about. Also, if you don't mind taking a few days to get your thoughts together, you might try carrying around a notebook to record your thoughts about the project so that you can peruse it for gems later. You may even write portions of the work ahead of time while you're inspired. You could even take a tape recorder and dictate your notes onto digital format for your use later. All of these ways can help you to get your notes down so you will have something to work from once you start writing.

With those notes in hand, you are ready to start writing. Someone once said if you want to write a book, you should go someplace boring. You may just want to go somewhere that you aren't likely to be interrupted repeatedly. This could be your home office, the local coffee shop, the library, or any number of places. Just choose a place where you can hear yourself think and get words down on either paper or screen. Unless it is a very short book, you will probably be writing it in more than one session, so you want your sessions to be as focused as they can be. That means no randomly surfing the Internet looking for more research or to play PopCap games. Settle yourself down and really focus on your writing.

In order to get your writing done, use the Pomodoro technique, a specific way of managing time to allow you to get a lot done. It requires you to work for 25 minutes and take a five-minute break, before starting to work again for another 25 minutes. Once you have done four segments of 25 minutes, you can take a longer break of 15-30 minutes. This is a useful way to structure your writing time. The Pomodoro technique uses a simple kitchen timer to keep track of the time you spend working or resting. You could easily adapt your phone's timer app for that purpose. There are also a myriad of Internet apps, which can be used for the same purpose such as Focus Booster. This technique can be used on any length of time that you want, so don't feel as if you have to go with the traditional 25 minutes. Set it for 30 minutes, an hour, an hour and a half - it's all up to you.

If you can sit for longer, then by all means, sit for longer. Just make sure you quit writing before you've completely lost steam for the day. If you find yourself rereading the same passage you've written over and over, you are done, no more usable writing is going to come out of you. The next time you have time to write, refer to your notes and the last bit that you wrote previously to get an idea of where you were and what the next step is. This can save you a lot of writing in circles as you get yourself together.

After you've put together your content, you want to ensure it is in the best shape possible for publication. This may mean hiring an editor or making a pass at editing yourself to ensure you are putting out a quality product. There's nothing quite as galling as suddenly realizing you have a typo in a printed manuscript. One way to go about editing is to think of it as several passes over the book. In the first pass, you should consider all the major things you want to change content-wise, including the placement of chapters and the viability of ideas. In the second pass, you should be looking for whether or not the entire thing holds together the way that you want it to. On the third and final pass, consider grammar mistakes and typos. You may wish to add a fourth pass to double-check your research for all the research you chose to use. Make sure all quotes are right and attributed and that the numbers are correct. One popular tip for editing is to print out the manuscript in its entirety and make your corrections on the paper copy so that you aren't changing and then rechanging things in your primary document.

Once you've edited to the best of your ability, or someone else's, then you are ready to format your book for publication. The formatting is different depending on the platform you're using, so refer to the following sections for how to format for Kindle Direct, CreateSpace, and Audiobook Creation Exchange.

Tip: If you already know what format you are going to use, set up to use that format from the beginning of the writing process. This eliminates having to reset your work into the format later on and can save you a serious headache.

If you write from paper to computer, you are going to be tempted to change things around to make them sound better - this is fine. You can and should make changes to your manuscript to make it sound its best.

If you find yourself needing to do more research, do it at a time that is not your writing time. Keep research and writing separate as much as possible so that you're not wasting writing time doing research or distracted by writing while trying to research.

Click here to check out the rest of How To Write A Book And Publish On Amazon on Amazon.

Or go to: http://amzn.to/1Hy83bC

MORE BOOKS FOR ENTREPRENEURS

Click here to check out the rest of <u>Entrepreneur Publishing's books on Amazon</u>.

Below you'll find some of my other popular books that are popular on Amazon and Kindle as well. Simply click on the links below to check them out. Alternatively, you can visit my author page on Amazon to see other work done by me.

<u>How Audiobooks Make You Smarter: 7 Little Known Ways Audio Books Can Boost Memory Capacity And Increase Intelligence</u>

<u>How To Write A Book And Publish On Amazon: Make Money With Amazon Kindle, CreateSpace And Audiobooks</u>

If the links do not work, for whatever reason, you can simply search for these titles on the Amazon website to find them.

Printed in Great Britain
by Amazon

41058530R00031